FAURÉ

Messe de Requiem

op. 48

Herausgegeben von / Edited by
Christina M. Stahl
und / and
Michael Stegemann

Partitur / Score

Bärenreiter Kassel · Basel · London · New York · Praha
BA 9461

INHALT / CONTENTS

BESETZUNG / ENSEMBLE

Soli: Soprano, Baryton

Chor / Chorus: Soprano, Alto, Ténor, Basse

Flûtes I, II, Clarinettes I, II, Bassons I, II;
Cors I–IV, Trompettes I, II, Trombones I–III; Timbales; Harpe;
Violons I, II, Altos I, II, Violoncelles I, II, Contrebasses; Orgue

Zu vorliegender Dirigierpartitur sind der Klavierauszug (BA 9461a)
und das Aufführungsmaterial (BA 9461) erhältlich.

In addition to the present full score, the vocal score (BA 9461a)
and the performance material (BA 9461) are also available.

Urtextausgabe aus: *Gabriel Fauré, Œuvres complètes*, Serie I, Band 2: *Messe de Requiem op. 48*
(Fassung von 1900) (BA 9461), vorgelegt von Christina M. Stahl und Michael Stegemann.

Urtext Edition taken from: *Gabriel Fauré, Œuvres complètes*, Series I, Volume 2: *Messe de Requiem op. 48*
(Version from 1900) (BA 9461), edited by Christina M. Stahl and Michael Stegemann.

VORWORT

Unmittelbar nach dem Abschluss seines Studiums an der Pariser „École Niedermeyer" – unter anderem bei Camille Saint-Saëns – hatte der 20-jährige Gabriel Fauré im Herbst 1865 einen Posten als Organist an der Basilique Saint-Sauveur in Rennes angetreten, wo er am 4. August 1866 sein erstes kirchenmusikalisches Werk zur Aufführung brachte: Den *Cantique de Jean Racine* op. 11. Im März 1870 wechselte er von Rennes zur Pariser Église Notre-Dame-de-Clignancourt; weitere Stationen seiner Laufbahn als Organist waren die Pariser Kirchen Saint-Honoré-d'Eylau (9. März bis Ende Juni 1871) und Saint-Sulpice (Oktober 1871 bis Januar 1874). In den nächsten Jahren vertrat er Saint-Saëns (während dessen Abwesenheiten) als Titular-Organist an der Église de la Madeleine. Mitte Mai 1877 übernahm Théodore Dubois Saint-Saëns' Posten; gleichzeitig wurde Fauré – auf Empfehlung von Saint-Saëns und Charles Gounod – zum *maître de chapelle* der Madeleine berufen. Am 2. Juni 1896 erfolgte schließlich seine Berufung zum Titular-Organisten der Kirche – ein Amt, das er gut neun Jahre lang innehatte. Sein letztes Konzert an der großen, 1845 installierten Cavaillé-Coll-Orgel der Madeleine gab Fauré am 1. Oktober 1905. Sein Nachfolger wurde der César-Franck-Schüler Henri Dallier.

Für diesen langen Zeitraum von vierzig Jahren, in denen Fauré als Kirchenmusiker tätig war, ist die Ausbeute an einschlägigen Kompositionen überraschend gering: Außer dem *Requiem* sind es lediglich die *Messe basse* und ein gutes Dutzend Motetten. Diese Zahl ist um so erstaunlicher, wenn man allein für Faurés Zeit an der Madeleine – einer der mondänsten Pfarreien von Paris – die Vielzahl der Gelegenheiten bedenkt, zu denen Musik unabdingbar war: Kirchenfeste und Feiertage, Hochzeiten und Beerdigungen. Sollte Fauré tatsächlich überwiegend fremde Werke zur Aufführung gebracht haben? Waren seine Orgeldienste und ‚auditions' ausschließlich improvisiert, da doch kein einziges Orgelwerk von ihm bekannt ist? Sind womöglich Werke – und wenn ja: welche und wie viele? – verloren gegangen, die er nicht für wert befunden hat, veröffentlicht zu werden? Einen Hinweis gibt vielleicht der Bericht des Kirchenmusikers Armand Vivet über die erste Aufführung des *Requiems* an der Madeleine im Januar 1888:

„Unmittelbar nach Ende der Zeremonie ließ der Pfarrer seinen Kapellmeister in die Sakristei rufen und machte ihm Vorhaltungen: ‚Was ist denn das für eine Totenmesse, die Sie da gerade haben singen lassen?' – ‚Nun, Herr Pfarrer, das ist ein *Requiem*, das ich komponiert habe.' – ‚Nun, Monsieur Fauré, wie brauchen dergleichen Neuheiten nicht; das Repertoire der Madeleine ist reichhaltig genug, beschränken Sie sich darauf.'"[1]

Denkbar ist also, dass Fauré tatsächlich angehalten wurde, die kirchenmusikalischen Darbietungen aus dem Fundus der Madeleine zu bestreiten. Fest steht immerhin, dass Fauré spätestens 1902 deutliche Anzeichen einer ‚Amts-Müdigkeit' zeigte, wie er Louis Aguettant gestand: „Seit so langer Zeit schon begleite ich an der Orgel Beerdigungs-Gottesdienste! Ich habe gründlich die Nase voll davon."[2]

Die Entstehung des *Requiems* fällt in die Zeit Faurés als *maître de chapelle* der Madeleine, wobei sich die Genese der einzelnen Teile und der verschiedenen Fassungen nur annähernd rekonstruieren lässt und aufgrund fehlender Quellen zahlreiche Fragen aufwirft. Der früheste Hinweis auf ein Requiem Faurés findet sich im Juni 1877 in einem Brief des Sängers Romain Bussine: „Ich habe gestern abend – er [i. e. Fauré; Anm. d. Übs.] hat mich nämlich besucht – ein ‚Libera me' für eine Totenmesse gehört, das absolut bezaubernd ist."[3] Die Formulierung „für eine Totenmesse" gibt zu denken: Sollte Fauré tatsächlich damals schon – plusminus einen Monat nach seiner Berufung an die Madeleine – die Komposition eines Requiems geplant haben? War die Vertonung des Responsoriums – mutmaßlich für Bariton und Orgel (die Partitur muss als verschollen gelten) – als Einzelstück für einen bestimmten Begräbnis-Gottesdienst gedacht, und wurde sie vielleicht sogar in einem solchen Kontext aufgeführt? Auch wenn die Fauré-Forschung bislang davon ausgeht, dass die kleine (Ur-)Fassung des *Requiems*

---

1 „Aussitôt terminée la cérémonie, M. le Curé fit appeler son maître de chapelle à la sacristie pour l'interpeller en ces termes: ‚Qu'est-ce donc que cette messe des morts que vous venez de faire chanter? – Mais, monsieur le Curé, c'est un *Requiem* de ma composition. – Voyons, monsieur Fauré, nous n'avons pas besoin de toutes ces nouveautés; le répertoire de la Madeleine est bien assez riche, contentez-vous-en.'" Armand Vivet: *La musique sacrée en France depuis la Révolution: Rétablissement, épanouissement, avenir*, in: *Congrès international de musique sacrée*, Paris (Desclée et Brouwer), S. 147ff.; zit. und übs. nach Jean-Michel Nectoux: *Gabriel Fauré. Les voix du clair-obscur*, Neuausgabe Paris (Fayard) 2008, S. 175.
2 „Voilà si longtemps que j'accompagne à l'orgue des services d'enterrements! J'en ai par-dessus la tête." Zit. und übs. nach Jean-Michel Nectoux: *Gabriel Fauré, op. cit.*, S. 164.
3 „J'ai entendu hier au soir, car il est venu me voir, un ‚Libera me' pour messe des morts qui est tout à fait charmant." Zit. und übs. nach Jean-Michel Nectoux: *Gabriel Fauré, op. cit.*, S. 176 Anm. 36.

zwischen Oktober 1887 und Januar 1888 entstanden ist, könnte Fauré doch Teile des Werkes bereits vorher komponiert und an der Madeleine aufgeführt haben.

Der nächste Hinweis sind drei im Sommer und Herbst 1887 entstandene Skizzenbücher, die Material zu den Sätzen *Introït et Kyrie, Hostias, Pie Jesu* und *Agnus Dei* enthalten, zum Teil noch in vom endgültigen d-Moll abweichenden Tonarten (c-Moll und h-Moll) notiert. Etwa zeitgleich beginnt Fauré im Oktober 1887 mit der Ausarbeitung des *Requiems* in jener unvollständigen und nur partiell orchestrierten Form, in der es am Montag, den 16. Januar 1888, an der Madeleine uraufgeführt wird: Ohne *Offertoire* und *Libera me*, und ohne Bläser. Anlass der Aufführung war ein feierliches Jahres-Seelenamt für den Architekten Joseph-Michel Le Soufaché.

Verschiedene Biographen haben die Entstehung des *Requiems* in den Kontext des Todes der Eltern des Komponisten gestellt; tatsächlich war Faurés Vater am 25. Juli 1885 gestorben, seine Mutter am 31. Dezember 1887. Auch der Komponist und Musikforscher Maurice Emmanuel scheint darauf angespielt zu haben, als er im März 1910 Fauré um einige Angaben zu Anlass und Uraufführung des *Requiems* bat. In seiner Antwort wies Fauré alle persönlichen Beweggründe für die Komposition zurück: „Cher Monsieur und lieber Freund, mein *Requiem* wurde *aus keinem besonderen Anlass* komponiert... zum Vergnügen, wenn ich so sagen darf!"[4]

Eine weitere Aufführung an der Madeleine am Freitag, den 4. Mai 1888, hatte vermutlich Faurés freundschaftliche Mäzenin Comtesse Élisabeth Greffulhe arrangiert und finanziert. Der Hinweis des Kritikers Camille Benoît auf eine „kurze Fanfare von Horn und Trompete"[5] im *Hosanna* beweist, dass dieses Mal die Orchesterbesetzung zumindest um die beiden Hörner und die beiden Trompeten erweitert worden war, die Fauré wohl von Anfang an vorgesehen und nachträglich in das Autograph eingetragen hatte.

Man muss wohl davon ausgehen, dass das *Requiem* in den nächsten vier, fünf Jahren mehrere weitere Aufführungen an der Madeleine erlebt hat, für die Fauré nach und nach weitere Ergänzungen und Verände-

rungen vornahm – nicht zuletzt im Hinblick auf eine geplante Veröffentlichung. So schreibt er am 24. Juni 1889 an die Comtesse Greffulhe: „Ich habe mich wieder an die Arbeit gesetzt und meinem *Requiem* ein Stück hinzugefügt: das *Offertoire*, das noch fehlte. Jetzt muss sich mein Verleger an die Arbeit machen!"[6] Auch das alte *Libera me* für Bariton und Orgel hat Fauré erst 1890 oder 1891 überarbeitet und als sechsten Satz hinzugefügt. Jedenfalls bildete das *Requiem* auch Bestandteil des Vertrages, den der Komponist am 16. September 1890 mit seinem Verleger Julien Hamelle abschloss. Hamelle war allerdings unglücklich über die eigenwillige Kammer-Fassung des Orchesters und drängte den Komponisten, für eine größere Verbreitung des Werkes die Besetzung zu erweitern. Es sollten freilich noch fast acht Jahre vergehen, bevor Fauré seinem Verleger in einem Brief vom 2. August 1898 versprach, „das *Requiem* druckfertig zu machen"[7].

Die Orchestration des *Requiems* war bis dahin wohl noch nicht über die nach und nach getätigten Hinzufügungen hinaus gediehen, so dass sich Fauré mit seinem Versprechen selbst unter erheblichen Druck gesetzt hatte. Das erste, was getan werden musste, war die Erstellung eines Klavierauszugs – eine Arbeit, die Fauré seinem Schüler Jean Roger-Ducasse übertrug. Was nun aber die eigentliche Orchestration betraf, so „scheint es, als habe der Komponist einige Mühe gehabt, seine Musik symphonisch zu konzipieren"[8]. Tatsächlich finden sich in seinem Œuvre nur verhältnismäßig wenige symphonische Werke, die zum Teil entweder kurz nach ihrer ersten Aufführung wieder zurückgezogen wurden oder aber gar nicht erst über ein erstes Skizzen-Stadium hinaus kamen. Bezeichnend ist zudem, dass Fauré die Orchestration mehrerer Werke nachweislich anderen Komponisten anvertraut hat: Charles Koechlin, Fernand Pécoud, Marcel Samuel-Rousseau – und eben Jean Roger-Ducasse. Es spricht tatsächlich manches dafür, dass auch die endgültige Fassung der Orchestration des *Requiems* ganz oder teilweise aus der Feder von Roger-Ducasse stammt, wenngleich Fauré sie zweifellos ‚abgesegnet' hat. In einem Brief an den belgischen Geiger, Dirigenten und Komponisten Eugène Ysaÿe hat Fauré im Vor-

---

4   „Cher Monsieur et ami Mon Requiem a été composé *pour rien... pour le plaisir, si j'ose dire!"* Gabriel Fauré an Maurice Emmanuel, [März 1910], zit. nach Jean-Michel Nectoux (Hg.), *Gabriel Fauré – Correspondance*, Paris (Flammarion) 1980, S. 139.
5   „courte fanfare de cor et trompette". Camille Benoît in *Le Guide musical*, 9.– 16. August 1888; zit. nach Jean-Michel Nectoux: *Notes critiques* zur Edition der Version 1893, Paris (J. Hamelle & Cie) 1994, S. VI.

6   „Je me suis remis au travail et j'ai ajouté à mon Requiem un morceau, l'Offertoire, qui manquait. C'est à mon éditeur, maintenant, de travailler!" Gabriel Fauré an die Comtesse Greffulhe, [24. Juni 1889], zit. nach Jean-Michel Nectoux (Hg.), *Gabriel Fauré – Correspondance, op. cit.*, S. 146.
7   „de mettre le *Requiem* en état de publication" Gabriel Fauré an Julien Hamelle, [2. August 1898], zit. nach *ibid.*, S. 232.
8   „Il semble que le musicien ait éprouvé quelque mal à penser sa musique en termes symphoniques." Jean-Michel Nectoux, *Gabriel Fauré, op. cit.*, S. 333.

feld der Brüsseler Erstaufführung die Besetzung der ‚großen' Fassung seines *Requiems* kommentiert:

„Die Orchestration stützt sich auf einen vierstimmigen Satz der geteilten Bratschen und Violoncelli. Es gibt keine 2. Violinen, und die 1. Violinen kommen erst ab dem *Sanctus* zum Einsatz (dem dritten Satz des *Requiems*). Um die Bratschen zu verstärken – je mehr es sind, desto besser – könntest Du die besten 2. Geiger bitten, für diese Aufführung Bratsche zu spielen. Desgleichen wäre es perfekt, wenn Du (ausnahmsweise) zwei Cellisten mehr als Deine übliche Zahl haben könntest. Davon abgesehen haben Blech- und Holzbläser nur sehr wenig zu tun, zumal die Orgel die ganze Zeit den Bläsersatz übernimmt."[9]

Am 6. April 1900 fand eine Amateur-Aufführung in der Salle industrielle in Lille mit 170 Ausführenden statt. Zwei Monate zuvor war bei Hamelle der gedruckte Klavierauszug von Roger-Ducasse erschienen, und die offizielle Erstaufführung der ‚großen' Fassung in Paris (am 12. Juli 1900) dürfte auch bereits festgestanden haben; so war dieses Konzert in Lille (in Anwesenheit des Komponisten) wohl so etwas wie eine ‚öffentliche Generalprobe' abseits der Hauptstadt. Die offizielle Erstaufführung der ‚großen' Fassung des *Requiems* fand dann am 12. Juli 1900 (nachmittags um 14.15 Uhr) in der gewaltigen, 5.000 Zuhörer fassenden Salle des fêtes des 1878 erbauten Pariser Palais du Trocadéro statt, als viertes der *Grands Concerts Officiels* der seit dem 15. April laufenden Weltausstellung. Unter der Leitung von Paul Taffanel spielten die vereinigten Orchester der Opéra und der Société des Concerts du Conservatoire, Marcel Samuel-Rousseau leitete den Chor; Solisten waren die Sopranistin Amélie Torrès und der Bassist Jean Vallier, die große, 66 Register umfassende Cavaillé-Coll-Orgel spielte Eugène Gigout. Mit 250 Mitwirkenden war die Besetzung noch größer als in Lille. Das Konzert wurde ein großer Erfolg und legte den Grundstein zu einer schnell und stetig wachsenden Zahl von Folgeaufführungen: „Man spielt mein *Requiem* in Brüssel, in Nancy, in Marseille, am Pariser Conservatoire! Sie werden sehen, ich werde noch ein berühmter Musiker!"[10]

Besonders gut ist die bereits erwähnte Aufführung dokumentiert, die Eugène Ysaÿe am 28. Oktober 1900 am Brüsseler Théâtre de l'Alhambra dirigierte. In ihrem Kontext existieren mehrere Briefe des Komponisten an Ysaÿe, die wertvolle Hinweise zur Besetzung und Interpretation des *Requiems* geben. So etwa am 4. August 1900:

„Eine Orgel wird erforderlich sein, da sie ununterbrochen begleitet, zur Not würde aber auch ein *lautes* Harmonium ausreichen.

Was die Größe des Chores betrifft, so hängt diese natürlich von der Größe des Saals ab, in dem Du Deine Konzerte veranstaltest. Das Werk dauert etwa *30 Minuten*, höchstens 35. Es ist (wie ich selbst!!) von durchweg *sanfter* Stimmung, und es verlangt *einen* nicht zu kräftigen Bass-Bariton – ein bisschen wie ein *Kantor* – und *einen* Sopran.

Die kleine Torrès musste im Trocadéro ihr Solo, das *Pie Jesu*, wiederholen. […] Der Bassist, *Vallier*, […] war entsetzlich: Ein richtiger Opern-Sänger, der nichts von der *Ruhe* und dem Ernst seines Parts in diesem Requiem verstanden hat."[11]

Amélie Torrès, die auch in Brüssel (und ein halbes Jahr später bei einer Aufführung des *Requiems* am Pariser Conservatoire) das Sopran-Solo sang, besaß offenbar genau jene ‚leichte' Stimme, die Fauré für das *Pie Jesu* vorschwebte; die *tessitura* der Partie (vom es' bis zum f") liegt allerdings so, dass auch ein Mezzosopran sie relativ mühelos bewältigen kann. Aufschlussreich ist auch Faurés negatives Urteil über Jean Vallier, das klare Direktiven für die Besetzung gibt: keine Opern-, sondern eher eine ‚Kantoren'-Stimme!

Ohne dass Fauré dies irgendwo ausdrücklich festgehalten hätte, gilt für die Solisten wie für den Chor, dass der lateinische Text nach den Regeln der gallikanischen Aussprache gesungen werden sollte, die in der französischen Kirchenmusik bis weit ins 20. Jahrhundert hinein die übliche Praxis darstellte.[12] Das

---

9 „L'orchestration est basée sur un quatuor d'altos et violoncelles divisés. Il n'y a pas de partie de 2d violon, et les premiers violons n'interviennent qu'à partir du *Sanctus* (3e numéro du *Requiem*). Pour engraisser les altos (plus il y en aura mieux ça vaudra) tu pourrais prier les meilleurs 2d violons de prendre des altos pour la circonstance. De même s'il était possible d'avoir deux violoncelles de plus que ton nombre habituel (par exception) ce serait parfait. A part cela les cuivres et les bois ont fort peu à faire, l'orgue remplissant l'harmonie tout le temps." Gabriel Fauré an Eugène Ysaÿe, 13. August [1900], zit. nach *ibid.*, S. 242.
10 „On joue mon *Requiem* à Bruxelles, et à Nancy, et à Marseille, et à Paris, au Conservatoire! Vous verrez que je vais devenir un musicien connu!" Gabriel Fauré an „Willy" [i. e. Henry Gautier-Villars], Oktober 1900, zit. nach *ibid.*, S. 179.
11 „Un orgue serait nécessaire car il accompagne tout le temps, mais à défaut un *fort* harmonium suffirait.
Quant au nombre des voix du chœur cela dépend naturellement des proportions de la salle où tu donnes tes Concerts. L'œuvre dure environ *30 minutes* ou 35 au plus. Elle est d'un caractère *doux* (comme moi-même!!) dans son ensemble, et elle nécessite *un* baryton-basse tranquille, un peu *chantre*, et *un* Soprano.
La petite Torrès s'est fait bisser au Trocadéro le morceau qu'elle avait à chanter, le *Pie Jesu*. […] Celui qui a chanté la basse, *Vallier*, […] a été détestable. C'est un vrai chanteur d'opéra qui n'a rien compris au *calme* et à la gravité de sa partie dans ce Requiem."
Gabriel Fauré an Eugène Ysaÿe, [4. August 1900], zit. nach Jean-Michel Nectoux (Hg.), *Gabriel Fauré – Correspondance, op. cit.*, S.240f.
12 Im Anschluss an seine Studie über Faurés *Requiem* hat sich der belgische Musikwissenschaftler Mutien-Omer Houziaux ausführlich mit diesem Problem auseinandergesetzt: *La prononciation*

heißt insbesondere, dass „u" grundsätzlich als [y] gesungen / ausgesprochen wird, mit entsprechend ‚französisierten' Konsonanten: *Requiem* als [rekyjɛm], *Jesu* als [ʒezy], *Sanctus* als [sãktys], *Dominus* als [dɔminys], *Deus* als [dɛys], und so weiter.

Faurés Hinweis, dass die Größe des Chores von der Größe des Aufführungsraumes abhängt, gilt auch für die Besetzung des Streicherapparats. Im Vorfeld der Trocadéro-Premiere gibt es ein Billett des Komponisten an Paul Taffanel: „Bernardel hat mir zugesagt, zur Probe am Samstag Morgen *10 Bratschen* herbeizuschaffen. Ob Sie wohl zehn 2. Geiger finden, die bereit wären, als Gelegenheits-Bratscher zu fungieren? Das wäre wunderbar!"[13] Dass damit zehn *zusätzliche* Bratschen gemeint sind, liegt nahe; immerhin waren an der Aufführung ja die Musiker zweier Pariser Orchester beteiligt. Und selbst für die (sicher kleiner besetzte) Brüsseler Aufführung rät der Komponist seinem Freund Ysaÿe, einige zweite Geiger als Bratscher einzusetzen, „um die Bratschen zu verstärken". Diese Brüsseler Aufführung kam beim Publikum und bei der Presse insgesamt sehr gut an, auch wenn die (von Fauré selbst erwähnte) *sanfte* Stimmung hier und da Irritationen auslöste. So bemerkte etwa der Rezensent der Zeitung *La Réforme*:

> „Für ein Werk der Trauer ist das *Requiem* von Monsieur E. [sic] Fauré kein allzu düsteres Werk. Es ist gefühlvoll, klagend und zart. Nichts von dem berühmten Heulen Bossuets oder dem Zähneklappern der Heiligen Schrift. Es bezaubert. Ein Requiem für Leute von Welt, die – gebildet und ein bisschen skeptisch – ihr Leben zu leben verstanden haben, so wie sie es nun verstehen, zu sterben."[14]

Das *Requiem* bleibt jedenfalls das Werk, in dem der Komponist seinem künstlerischen Credo vielleicht am nächsten gekommen ist: „Die Kunst, und vor allem die Musik, hat für mich vor allem die Aufgabe, uns so weit wie möglich über die Wirklichkeit hinaus zu heben."[15]

*

Die vorliegende Dirigierpartitur beruht auf der kritischen Neuausgabe, die im Rahmen der *Œuvres Complètes de Gabriel Fauré* veröffentlicht wurde; sie stützt sich im Wesentlichen auf die folgenden Quellen:

A Teil-Autograph der Partitur (F-Pn, Ms. 410 – 413) mit den Sätzen *Introït et Kyrie*, *Sanctus*, *Agnus Dei* und *In paradisum*.

Ma Autographes Stimmen-Material Gabriel Faurés aus dem Besitz der Madeleine (F-Pn, Ms. 17717).

Mc Handschriftliches Stimmen-Material mehrerer Kopisten aus dem Besitz der Madeleine (F-Pn, Rés. Vma. ms. 891 & 892).

Ré Erstausgabe des von Jean Roger-Ducasse erstellten Klavierauszugs, veröffentlicht im Februar 1900 von Julien Hamelle (Plattennummer: J. 4531. H.). Das verwendete Exemplar (F-Pn, Rés. Vmb. 49) enthält zahlreiche autographe Korrekturen Faurés.

E Erstausgabe der Orchesterpartitur, veröffentlicht im September 1901 von Julien Hamelle (Plattennummer: J. 4650. H.); verwendetes Exemplar: F-Pn, Vma. 1938.

Mé Erstausgabe des Stimmen-Materials, veröffentlicht von Julien Hamelle im September 1901 (Plattennummer: J. 4651. H.); verwendetes Exemplar: F-Prt (Bibliothèque des orchestres), T 159.

Christina M. Stahl
Michael Stegemann
Herne / Paris, Oktober 2010

---

gallicane du chant latin garante d'authenticité?, in: *Revue de la Société liégeoise de Musicologie*, 20 / 2002, S. 3–121.

13 „Bernardel m'a répondu qu'il ferait porter *10 Altos* pour la répétition de samedi matin! Trouverez-vous dix 2[ds] violons qui consentent à devenir altistes d'occasion? Ce serait superbe!" Gabriel Fauré an Paul Taffanel, [6. Juli 1900], zit. nach Jean-Michel Nectoux, *Préface*, in: Mutien-Omer Houziaux: *A la recherche "des" Requiem de Fauré*, Liège / Paris (Société liégeoise de musicologie / Librairie Klincksieck) 2000, S. xviii.

14 „Le *Requiem* de M. E. [sic] Fauré, pour être une œuvre funèbre, n'a rien de trop lugubre. Elle est sentimentale, plaintive et délicate. Rien du fameux pleur de Bossuet ni du grincement de dents des Écritures. Elle charme. C'est un Requiem pour gens du monde, lettrés, un peu sceptiques, et qui après avoir eu du savoir vivre ont aussi fait preuve de savoir mourir." Zit. nach *ibid.*, S. 153.

15 „Pour moi l'art, la musique surtout, consiste à nous élever le plus loin possible au-dessus de ce qui est." Gabriel Fauré an seinen Sohn Philippe, [31. August] 19[08], in: Jean-Michel Nectoux (Hg.), *Gabriel Fauré – Correspondance, op. cit.*, S. 275.

PREFACE

No sooner had he completed his studies at the École Niedermeyer in Paris – including with Camille Saint-Saëns – than the 20-year-old Gabriel Fauré took up a post as organist at the Basilique Saint-Sauveur in Rennes in the autumn of 1865, where on 4 August 1866 he performed his first church-music work: the *Cantique de Jean Racine* op. 11. In March 1870 he changed from Rennes to Paris's Église Notre-Dame-de-Clignancourt; other stages of his career as an organist saw him at the Paris churches of Saint-Honoré-d'Eylau (9 March to the end of June 1871) and Saint-Sulpice (October 1871 to January 1874). In the following few years he stood in for Saint-Saëns (during his absence) as titular organist at the Église de la Madeleine before Théodore Dubois took over Saint-Saëns's post in the middle of May 1877 and at the same time Fauré – on the recommendation of Saint-Saëns and Charles Gounod – was appointed *maître de chapelle* of the Madeleine. His appointment as titular organist of the church – an office which he held for a good nine years – finally came on 2 June 1896. Fauré gave his last concert at the grand Cavaillé-Coll organ of the Madeleine, installed in the church in 1845, on 1 October 1905. His successor was the César-Franck pupil Henri Dallier.

Given that Fauré worked as a church musician for forty years, his output of church-music compositions during this long period was surprisingly small: apart from the *Requiem* there are only the *Messe basse* and a good dozen motets. This figure is all the more astonishing if we but consider for Fauré's time at the Madeleine alone – one of the most fashionable parishes in Paris – the great number of occasions for which music was indispensable: church festivals and religious holidays, weddings and funerals. Are we to believe that Fauré actually performed mainly other composers' works? With there in point of fact being no knowledge of one single organ work by him, were his organ duties and "auditions" entirely improvised? Might works have been lost which he did not consider worthy of publication, and if so, which and how many? We do not know; nor does any of the literature on Fauré furnish any snippets of information to enlighten us. A possible clue is provided by the report of the church musician Armand Vivet on the first performance of the *Requiem* at the Madeleine in January 1888:

"As soon as the ceremony had finished, the parish priest summoned his Master of the Chapel to the sacristy and remonstrated with him: 'What sort of requiem mass is that which you have just had sung?' – 'Well, Father, it is a *Requiem* which I have composed.' – 'Well, Monsieur Fauré, we do not need novelties of that kind; the repertoire of the Madeleine is rich enough, so be content with it.'"[1]

It is thus conceivable that Fauré was obliged to use the resources of the Madeleine for the church music performances. What is certain, however, is that Fauré was showing distinct signs of jadedness from holding office by 1902, as he admitted to Louis Aguettant: "I've been accompanying funeral services on the organ for such a long time now! I'm really fed up to the back teeth with it all."[2]

It was while he was *maître de chapelle* of the Madeleine that Fauré composed the Requiem. The genesis of the individual parts and the various versions can be only roughly reconstructed, however, and because of missing sources it raises numerous questions. The earliest indication of a *Requiem* by Fauré is to be found in June 1877 in a letter written by the singer Romain Bussine: "Yesterday evening I heard – for he [i. e. Fauré; added by the translator] came to see me – a 'Libera me' for a requiem mass which is utterly enchanting."[3] The formulation "for a requiem mass" ("*pour messe des morts*") gives reason to stop and think: are we to believe that at the time – give or take a month after being appointed to his post at the Madeleine – Fauré was in fact already planning to compose a requiem? Was the setting of the responsory – probably for baritone and organ (the score must be presumed lost) – meant to be an isolated piece for a specific funeral service, and might it even have been performed in such circumstances? Even if Fauré scholarship has hitherto presumed that the small (original) version of the *Requiem* was written between October 1887 and January 1888, Fauré could nevertheless have already composed parts of the work before that and performed them at the

1   For the original french text see the Vorwort, p. III. Armand Vivet: *La musique sacrée en France depuis la Révolution: Rétablissement, épanouissement, avenir*, in: *Congrès international de musique sacrée*, Paris (Desdée et Brouwer), p. 147ff; quoted and translated from Jean-Michel Nectoux: *Gabriel Fauré. Les voix du clair-obscur*, Reprint Paris (Fayard) 2008, p. 175.
2   Quoted and translated from Jean-Michel Nectoux: *Gabriel Fauré, op. cit.*, p. 164.
3   Quoted and translated from *ibid.*, p. 176, note 36.

Madeleine. The next clue is provided by three sketch-books from the summer and autumn of 1887 containing material for the movements *Introït et Kyrie, Hostias, Pie Jesu* and *Agnus Dei,* and in part still notated in keys different to the final D minor (C minor and B minor). Roughly at the same time, in October 1887, Fauré begins putting the *Requiem* into the incomplete and only partially orchestrated form in which it is given its first performance on Monday, 16 January 1888, in the Madeleine: without *Offertoire* and *Libera me,* and without any wind instruments. The performance was to celebrate an annual requiem mass for the architect Joseph-Michel Le Soufaché.

Various biographers have put the genesis of the *Requiem* in the context of the death of the composer's parents; Fauré's father did in fact die on 25 July 1885, his mother on 31 December 1887. The composer and musicologist Maurice Emmanuel also seems to have had this in mind when he asked Fauré in March 1910 for some details about the reason for and the première of the *Requiem.* In his answer Fauré denied having any personal motives for composing the work: "Cher Monsieur and dear friend, my *Requiem* was composed *for nothing in particular... for fun,* if I may be permitted to say so!" [4]

It is likely to have been Fauré's kindly patron Comtesse Élisabeth Greffulhe who arranged and financed a further performance at the Madeleine on Friday, 4 May 1888. The fact that the critic Camille Benoît mentioned a "short fanfare of horn and trumpet"[5] in the *Hosanna* shows that the orchestral forces had this time been augmented by at least the two horns and the two trumpets which Fauré had no doubt been intending to include from the very beginning and had subsequently added to the score.

It is reasonable to assume that the *Requiem* was performed on several other occasions at the Madeleine in the following four to five years, with Fauré successively making further additions and changes to them each time – not least with an eye to a planned publication. He writes, for example, to the Comtesse Greffulhe on 24 June 1889: "I have set to work again and added a piece to my *Requiem,* the *Offertoire,* which was still missing. It's now up to my publisher to get down

to work."[6] It was not until 1890 or 1891 that Fauré also reworked the old *Libera me* for baritone and organ and added it as the sixth movement. At all events the *Requiem* also formed part of the contract the composer concluded with his publisher Julien Hamelle on 16 September 1890. Hamelle was unhappy, however, about the unconventional chamber version of the orchestra and urged the composer to enlarge the scoring in order that the work may reach a wider public. Yet nearly eight years were to pass before Fauré promised his publisher in a letter dated 2 August 1898 "to prepare the *Requiem* for publication"[7].

By that time the orchestration of the *Requiem* had evidently not yet progressed beyond the additions he had gradually been making, and Fauré had thus put himself under considerable pressure with his promise. What needed to be done first was to prepare a piano reduction – a job which Fauré gave to his pupil Jean Roger-Ducasse. As far as the actual orchestration was concerned, however, "it seems as if the composer had some difficulties thinking of his music in symphonic terms".[8] And in his œuvre there are indeed only relatively few symphonic works to be found, some of which were withdrawn again shortly after their first performance or did not even progress beyond an initial sketching stage. What is significant too, is the fact that Fauré is known to have entrusted other composers with the orchestration of several works: Charles Koechlin, Fernand Pécoud, Marcel Samuel-Rousseau – and even Jean Roger-Ducasse. There is actually evidence to suggest that even the final version of the *Requiem's* orchestration was penned in its entirety or in part by Roger-Ducasse, albeit with Fauré's undoubted "blessing". In a letter to the Belgian violinist, conductor and composer Eugène Ysaÿe, Fauré commented on the scoring of the 'grand' version of his *Requiem* prior to its première in Brussels:

"The orchestration is based on a quartet of divided violas and cellos. There aren't any 2nd violins, and the 1st violins do not enter until the *Sanctus* (the third movement of the *Requiem*). To reinforce the violas (the more there are, the better), could you ask the best 2nd violinists to play the viola for this performance. If you could also have two cellists more than your usual number (just this once), it would be perfect. Apart from that the brass and wood-

4   Gabriel Fauré to Maurice Emmanuel, [March 1910], quoted from Jean-Michel Nectoux (ed.), *Gabriel Fauré – Correspondance,* Paris (Flammarion) 1980, p. 139.
5   Camille Benoît in *Le Guide musical,* 9 – 16 August 1888; quoted from Jean-Michel Nectoux: *Notes critiques on the edition of the 1893 version,* Paris (J. Hamelle & Cie) 1994, p. VI.

6   Gabriel Fauré to the Comtesse Greffulhe, [24 June 1889], quoted from Jean-Michel Nectoux (ed.), *Gabriel Fauré – Correspondance, op. cit.,* p. 146.
7   Gabriel Fauré to Julien Hamelle, [2 August 1898], quoted from *ibid.,* p. 232.
8   Jean-Michel Nectoux, *Gabriel Fauré, op. cit.,* p. 333.

wind have very little to do, especially as the organ plays the wind parts the whole time."[9]

170 amateur musicians gave a performance of the work in the Salle industrielle in Lille on 6 April 1900. The printed piano score prepared by Roger-Ducasse had been published by Hamelle two months before and in all likelihood the official first performance of the 'grand' version in Paris (on 12 July 1900) would have already been arranged as well. This concert in Lille, which the composer attended, was thus probably something like a 'public final rehearsal' away from the capital. It was then on 12 July 1900 (at a quarter past two in the afternoon) in the enormous 5,000-capacity Salles des fêtes of Paris's Palais du Trocadéro built in 1878 that the official première performance of the 'grand' version of the *Requiem* took place as the fourth of the *Grands Concerts Officiels* of the World Fair, which had been running since 15 April. The combined orchestras of the Opéra and the Société des Concerts du Conservatoire played under the baton of Paul Taffanel, Marcel Samuel-Rousseau conducted the choir, the soloists were the soprano Amélie Torrès and the bass Jean Vallier, and Eugène Gigout was at the great, 66-stop Cavaillé-Coll organ. With 250 musicians performing, the forces were even larger than in Lille. The concert was a huge success and laid the foundations for a rapidly and continually growing number of subsequent performances: "One plays my *Requiem* in Brussels, and in Nancy, and in Marseille, and in Paris, at the Conservatoire! You will see that I shall become a famous musician!"[10]

The performance mentioned above conducted by Eugène Ysaÿe in Brussels' Théâtre de l'Alhambra on 28 October 1900 is particularly well documented, with several of the composer's letters to Ysaÿe having survived and providing valuable information on the instrumentation and interpretation of the *Requiem*. In a letter dated 4 August 1900, for instance, Fauré wrote:

"An organ would be necessary because it accompanies the whole way through, but failing that a *loud* harmonium would do.

As for the number of voices in the choir, that will naturally depend on the size of the hall where you give your concerts. The work lasts about *30 minutes* or 35 at the most. Altogether, it is (like myself!!) of a *gentle* character and it calls for *one* quiet bass-baritone, a little like a cantor, and *one* soprano.

Little Torrès was encored at the Trocadéro for the piece she had to sing, the *Pie Jesu*. [...] The man who sang the bass part, *Vallier*, [...] was dreadful – a real opera singer who understood nothing of the *composure* and gravity of his part in this Requiem."[11]

Amélie Torrès, who also sang the soprano solo in Brussels (and six months later at a performance of the *Requiem* at the Paris Conservatoire), apparently had precisely that "light" voice which Fauré had in mind for the *Pie Jesu*; the tessitura of the part (ranging from e' flat to f") is such, however, that even a mezzo-soprano can manage it with relatively little difficulty. What is also rather telling is Fauré's clear directions for the part, revealing his negative opinion of Jean Vallier: "not an operatic but rather a 'cantor' voice!"

Although Fauré did not explicitly specify it anywhere, both the soloists and the choir are expected to sing the Latin text according to the rules of Gallican pronunciation, which was the customary practice in French church music until well into the 20th century.[12] This means in particular that "u" is always sung/pronounced as [y], with correspondingly 'Gallicized' consonants: *Requiem* as [rekyjɛm], *Jesu* as [ʒezy], *Sanctus* as [sãktys], *Dominus* as [dɔminys], *Deus* as [dɛys], and so on.

Fauré's comment that the number of voices in the choir will depend on the size of the hall also applies to the make-up of the strings. In a letter written to Paul Taffanel ahead of the Trocadéro première the composer says: "Bernardel has promised to get *10 violas* for the rehearsal on Saturday morning! Whether you can perhaps find ten second violinists who would agree to being occasional viola players? That would be wonderful!"[13] It stands to reason that ten *additional* violas are meant; after all, the musicians of two Paris orchestras were involved in the performance. And even for the (surely smaller-scale) Brussels performance the composer advises his friend Ysaÿe to use some second violinists as viola players "to reinforce the violas". All in all, this performance in Brussels was very well received by the audience and the press, even if the *gentle* character (mentioned by Fauré him-

9 Gabriel Fauré to Eugène Ysaÿe, 13 August [1900], quoted from *ibid.*, p. 242.
10 Gabriel Fauré to "Willy" [i. e. Henry Gautier-Villars], October 1900, quoted from *ibid.*, p. 179.

11 Gabriel Fauré to Eugène Ysaÿe, [4 August 1900], quoted from Jean-Michel Nectoux (ed.), *Gabriel Fauré – Correspondance, op. cit.*, p. 240f.
12 After his study on Fauré's *Requiem* the Belgian musicologist Mutien-Omer Houziaux delved into this problem in detail: *La prononciation gallicane du chant latin garante d'authenticité?*, in *Revue de la Société liégeoise de Musicologie*, 20/2002, pp. 3–121.
13 Gabriel Fauré to Paul Taffanel, [6 July 1900], quoted from Jean-Michel Nectoux, *Préface*, in Mutien-Omer Houziaux: *À la recherche »des« Requiem de Fauré*, Liège/Paris (Société liégeoise de musicologie / Librairie Klincksieck) 2000, p. xviii.

self) caused some confusion here and there. The critic of the newspaper *La Réforme* observed, for example:

> "For a funeral work, the *Requiem* of Monsieur E. [*sic*] Fauré is not all that sombre. It is sentimental, plaintive and delicate. Nothing of the famous wailing of Bossuet or the gnashing of teeth of the Holy Scriptures. It charms. It is a Requiem for people of the world who – cultured and a little sceptical – have understood how to live their life, just as they now know how to die."[14]

The *Requiem* certainly remains the work in which the composer perhaps came closest to his artistic credo: "To my mind, art, and above all music, consists in lifting us as far as possible above what is."[15]

*

This score is based on the critical new edition, which was published as part of the *Œuvres Complètes de Gabriel Fauré* and draws predominantly upon the following sources:

A Partial autograph of the score (F-Pn, Ms. 410 – 413) with the movements *Introït et Kyrie, Sanctus, Agnus Dei* and *In paradisum*.

---

14 Quoted from *ibid.*, p. 153.
15 Gabriel Fauré to his son Philippe, [31 August] 19[08], in: Jean-Michel Nectoux (ed.), *Gabriel Fauré – Correspondance, op. cit.*, p. 275.

Ma Autograph part material of Gabriel Fauré from the Madeleine's collection (F-Pn, Ms. 17717).
Mc Manuscript part material of several copyists from the Madeleine's collection (F-Pn, Rés. Vma. ms. 891 & 892).
Ré First edition of the piano reduction edited by Jean Roger-Ducasse, published in February 1900 by Julien Hamelle (plate number: J. 4531. H.). The copy used (F-Pn, Rés. Vmb. 49) contains numerous autograph corrections by Fauré.
E First edition of the orchestral score published in September 1901 by Julien Hamelle (plate number: J. 4650. H.); copy used: F-Pn, Vma. 1938.
Mé First edition of the part material published by Julien Hamelle in September 1901 (plate number: J. 4651. H.); copy used: F-Prt (Bibliothèque des orchestres), T 159.

Christina M. Stahl
Michael Stegemann
Herne/Paris, October 2010
(*Translation: Steve Taylor*)

ZUR EDITION

Das grundlegende Prinzip der *Gabriel Fauré Oeuvres Complètes* ist es, der Fassung letzter Hand des Komponisten zu folgen, d. h. die zahlreichen Revisionen oder Ergänzungen, die im Stadium des Stichs für die erste oder zweite Auflage hinzugefügt wurden oder in seinen persönlichen Druckexemplaren in Form handschriftlicher Korrekturen konserviert sind, werden übernommen. Um den musikalischen Text nicht unnötig zu überfrachten, sind die Ergänzungen der Herausgeber bei Dynamik und Akzidenzien in Kleinstich wiedergegeben, ⎯ und ⎯-Zeichen sowie Phrasierungsbögen (ergänzte wie versetzte) sind durch eine dünne Durchstreichung kenntlich gemacht. Alle weiteren herausgeberischen Eingriffe sind in eckigen Klammern notiert.

EDITORIAL NOTES

The fundamental principle of *Gabriel Fauré Oeuvres Complètes* is to follow the composer's last stance on his work; in other words, we adopt the numerous revisions or small additions made at the engraving stage preceding the first or second edition or preserved in the form of handwritten corrections in his personal copies of his printed scores. In order to avoid an unnecessarily busy musical text, editorial amendments in terms of dynamics and accidentals are given in small print, ⎯ and ⎯ markings, added or moved phrasing slurs are indicated with a slash. All other editorial amendments are written in square brackets.

Messe de Requiem

op. 48

I Introït et Kyrie

4

Tenor: et lux per-pe - tu-a lu - ce - at e - - is.

*) Erstausgabe und Orchestermaterial: Streicher, Orgel —————— ab dem 2. Schlag bis zum Taktende **p** vom 1. Schlag in Takt 37, zweifellos ein Fehler; verbessert nach dem Klavierauszug. / First edition and orchestral material: strings, organ —————— from the 2nd beat until the end of the bar, **p** from the 1st beat of bar 37, without doubt a mistake; corrected according to the vocal score.

*) Fagott II, Takte 51, 53: fehlen in der gedruckten Partitur, vervollständigt nach der gedruckten Instrumentalstimme. Takt 53: 3. Note notiert als *f* statt *e* ♯./
Bassoon II, bars 51, 53: missing in the published score, restored according to the published orchestral part. Bar 53: the 3rd note notated as *f* instead of *e* ♯.

8

*) Fagott II, Takte 72, 74: fehlen in der gedruckten Partitur, vervollständigt nach der gedruckten Instrumentalstimme. / Bassoon II, bars 72, 74: missing in the published score, restored according to the published orchestral part.

*) Chor, Takte 81–82: gedruckte Partitur und Klavierauszug "eleison" mit Überbindung vom 2. Schlag in Takt 81 zum 1. Schlag in Takt 82. Die OCGF folgt der autographen Version und stellt die notwendige Repetition von "Kyrie [eleison]" wieder her. / Chorus, bars 81-82: published score and vocal score "eleison" with tie phrasing from the 2nd beat of bar 81 to the 1st beat of bar 82. The OCGF follows autograph version and thus re-establishes the necessary repetition of "Kyrie [eleison]".

14

II Offertoire

E

III Sanctus

IV Pie Jesu

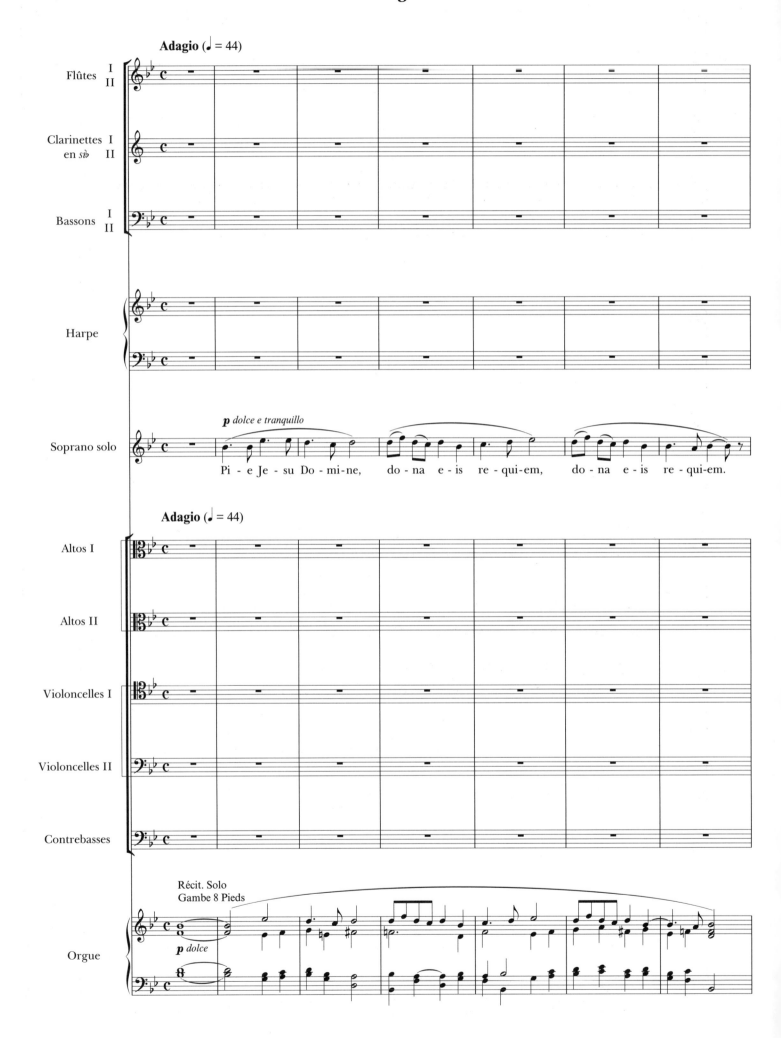

do - na_ e - is, do - na_ e - is sem - pi - ter - nam re - qui - em, sem - pi - ter - nam re - qui - em.

V Agnus Dei

*) Metronomangabe ♩ = 69 im Autograph und in der Partitur; fehlt im Orchestermaterial; geändert nach dem Klavierauszug und in Angleichung mit Takt 88. / Metronome marking ♩ = 69 in the autograph and the score; missing in the orchestral material; changed according to the vocal score and to agree with bar 88.

48

*) Eine Angleichung der Divergenzen zwischen dem ♯ der Soprane, Altos, Tenöre, Violinen und Violen einerseits und dem ♭ der Bässe, Violoncelli, Kontrabässe und der Orgel andererseits hätte solch gravierende Änderungen im Notentext erfordert, dass die OCGF sich für die Beibehaltung von Fauré's (en)harmonischer Notation entschieden hat, auch wenn dies Verwirrung stiften sollte. / A modification of the divergence between the ♯ of the sopranos, altos, tenors, violins and violas on one side and the ♭ of the basses, violoncellos, double basses and organ on the other would have required such a substantial change to the musical text that the OCGF has opted to maintain Fauré's (en)harmonic notation which is found in all the sources, even though it could cause some confusion.

G

H

VI Libera me

56

62

64

G

J

73

VII In paradisum